Witness to History

World War I

Sean Connolly

H. www.heinemann.co.uk/library

Visit our website to find out more information about **Heinemann Library** books.

To order:

☎ Phone 44 (0) 1865 888066

🗎 Send a fax to 44 (0) 1865 314091

💻 Visit the Heinemann Bookshop at www.heinemann.co.uk/library to browse our catalogue and order online.

First published in Great Britain by Heinemann Library, Halley Court, Jordan Hill, Oxford OX2 8EJ, part of Harcourt Education. Heinemann is a registered trademark of Harcourt Education Ltd.

Editorial: Sarah Eason and Kathy Peltan
Design: Ron Kamen and Celia Floyd
Illustrations: Jeff Edwards, Stefan Chabluk
Picture Research: Maria Joannou
Production: Viv Hichens

Originated by Ambassador Litho Ltd
Printed and bound in Hong Kong/China by South China Printing

ISBN 0 431 17032 0 (hardback)
07 06 05 04 03
10 9 8 7 6 5 4 3 2 1

ISBN 0 431 17038 X (paperback)
08 07 06 05 04
10 9 8 7 6 5 4 3 2 1

British Library Cataloguing in Publication Data
Connolly, Sean, 1956–
  World War I. – (Witness to History)
  1. World War, 1914–1918 – Juvenile literature
  I. Title
  940.3

A full catalogue record for this book is available from the British Library.

Acknowledgements
The publishers would like to thank the following for permission to reproduce photographs:
AKG p.36; Art Archive p.12; Corbis p.44; Hulton Archive pp.5, 15, 17, 22, 24, 31, 34, 35, 42, 46, 48; John Frost Newspapers p 7; Photos12.com p 38; Popperfoto pp 26, 28, 51; Popperfoto/Reuters p.6; Tank Museum, Bovington p.4; Topham Picturepoint pp.10, 18, 25, 41, 49, (John Giles) 50; unknown pp. 14, 32.

Cover photograph of a soldier in a trench, reproduced with permission of Topham.

The publishers would like to thank Faber & Faber for permission to print the poem 'Aftermath' by Siegfield Sassoon, which appears on page 43.

The publishers would like to thank Bob Rees, historian and Assistant Head Teacher, for his assistance in the preparation of this book.

Words appearing in bold, like **this,** are explained in the Glossary.

Contents

Introduction

World War I (1914–1918) was a turning point in world history. No previous conflict could match its scale of destruction. Millions of people died, often in battles that seemed to have no winners or losers – only dead and wounded. World War I was the first conflict to use modern technology on a wide scale. Armies and navies kept contact with radio and telegraph, while cars and trucks linked up with trains to move troops around. Modern industrial methods produced big guns that could send shells more than 15 km (9 miles). Submarines, aeroplanes, **airships** and tanks also made their first appearance in combat during the war. Hand grenades and barbed wire – all used for the first time as weapons during World War I – added to these deadly developments.

The most striking image of World War I is that of the trenches. On the great battlefields, huge armies lay in waiting, unable to advance against each other. Soldiers on each side dug long trenches. There, in the damp, muddy soil, they were forced to live with the constant noise of gunfire.

Power struggles

At the time, World War I was known simply as 'the Great War'. It was a struggle between Europe's great powers, grouped into two opposing **alliances**. On one side were the **Central Powers** (led by Germany, Austria-Hungary, Bulgaria and Turkey known, at the time, as the Ottoman Empire). Facing them in the war were the **Allied Powers** (led by Great Britain and its **Empire**, France, Belgium, Russia, Italy and the United States). Overall, more than 65 million soldiers fought in the war.

The tank, a British invention used for the first time in World War I, was designed to cross muddy battlefields while gunning down the enemy.

The alliances that developed in the decades before the war created a spider's web of promises and pledges between countries. When the heir to the throne of Austria-Hungary was killed by a Serbian **nationalist** in June 1914, the complicated network of alliances forced European leaders into conflict. There seemed to be no stopping a war. Within five weeks, the continent had been plunged into the nightmarish conflict that would last more than four years.

The long haul

At first, both sides believed that the fighting would be 'over by Christmas', but World War I settled into a long, deadly conflict. Millions of men died in its most famous battles, such as the Marne, Ypres, the Somme and Verdun, yet these battles produced very few obvious gains. In the end, the war turned into a contest of strength and staying power. When the United States entered the war in 1917 – its first involvement in a European conflict – the Allied Powers gained the upper hand. The war began to turn in their favour and, a little more than a year later, the Central Powers were forced to surrender.

German Kaiser Wilhelm II of Germany with his cousin Tsar Nicholas of Russia. On August 1 1914, Germany declared war on Russia.

When the fighting was finally over, no one could be certain how many had been killed, but historians estimate that up to 10 million men lost their lives on the battlefield – and that another 20 million were wounded. After it ended, world leaders tried to describe World War I as 'the war to end all wars'. Little did they know that another conflict would claim even more lives a little more than two decades later.

How do we know?

By studying history, we can learn about the events of the past. If, for example, we need to find out about Alexander the Great or Napoleon's defeat at Waterloo, we can find many books and articles about these subjects. They can tell us when and how these events took place, as well as who were the leading characters. They will often explain why things have happened, by giving the background to the events, and they will also describe how the events themselves changed the course of history.

Although these works are helpful and informative, they are often written many years (sometimes many centuries) after the events they describe. Like any story that is told, some changes can creep into the accounts. Perhaps the historian did not like French people, or Greeks, or military leaders generally. Such an attitude of mind can affect how the story gets told, because the historian wants to present the facts as he or she would have liked them to occur. Perhaps the historian might leave out some of the facts that do not fit into this view of the world. This type of personal opinion is called **bias**, and it makes some historical accounts unreliable.

Of course, a historian might have no personal opinion on the matter, but he or she may still use other accounts that were written long after the events occurred. Such accounts are called **secondary sources**, because the historian arrives at them second-hand. Here again, we must take care in deciding on the truth. The second historian, basing his or her history on earlier retellings, might be repeating the bias, or even mistakes, of the previous accounts. Each retelling increases the risk of bias and inaccuracy.

Today, war reporters bring us details and pictures of conflicts around the world almost as they are happening.

Getting to the source

This book aims to use **primary sources** to tell the story of World War I. These are the first-hand accounts of events. Historians dealing with events of long ago must rely on written primary sources: codes of law, parish registers, letters and, sometimes, journals or diaries. World War I is a much more recent event and there are some people alive today who lived through the period. So historians can use a much wider range of primary sources to get at the truth of this story. Tape recordings, on-line interviews and film footage of events add to the wealth of written material about this terrible war.

Making our minds up

Of course, not every primary source is without bias, and that is true of some of the sources you will find in this book. Personal diaries and accounts tell the truth, but only so far as the writer can know it. The diary accounts of Gallipoli (see page 23) and the Irish Rebellion (see page 29) were written by ordinary people who had no part to play in the planning of World War I. Other accounts, although written by eyewitnesses, were meant to urge their country to victory. The Red Baron's account of his flying triumphs (see page 25) and the US reporter's account of fighting in Europe (see page 35) are examples of such **propaganda**. By recognizing the shortcomings of such primary sources, we can judge them and use them wisely in order to piece together the complicated jigsaw puzzle that is World War I.

The news that war had broken out created a sense of excitement across much of Europe.

Alliances and crises

From the late nineteenth century, and into the twentieth, Europe became tense and watchful. A growing sense of **nationalism** led each country to try to gain further power – often at the expense of other nations. European countries competed for **colonies**, especially in places that were rich in raw materials that were so important for industry. There was an atmosphere of mistrust, and many European nations began spending a lot of money to build up their armies and navies.

Because of this sense of mistrust (and the military build-up), nations sought **alliances** with other powers. They usually argued that the alliances were a way of defending themselves, but these European nations were actually sowing the seeds for war with a series of promises to fight. Gradually, these alliances drew in more and more countries, until there were two hostile military alliances: the **Triple Alliance** (Germany, Austria-Hungary and Italy) and the **Triple Entente** (Great Britain, France and Russia). Shifts within these alliances – when countries changed sides if they sensed new dangers close to home – added to the growing sense of crisis.

Key
Triple Entente (The Allies)
Triple Alliance (Central Powers)
Turkey joined the Central Powers in October 1914. Italy joined the Allies in 1915.

A series of treaties and alliances seemed to change the face of Europe in the late nineteenth century. Mistrust and suspicion led nations to group themselves into two opposing sides.

An alliance is made

Many of the agreements made between European governments were secret, although they locked the countries involved into complicated promises. This is an excerpt from the Franco-Russian Alliance Military **Convention**. It was signed on 18 August 1892, but was not made public until 1918.

France and Russia, being moved by a common desire to preserve peace have agreed upon the following provisions:

1. If France is attacked by Germany, or by Italy supported by Germany, Russia shall employ all her available forces to attack Germany. If Russia is attacked by Germany, or by Austria supported by Germany, France shall employ all her available forces to attack Germany.

2. In case the forces of the Triple Alliance, or of any one of the Powers belonging to it, should be **mobilized**, France and Russia shall mobilize immediately and simultaneously the whole of their forces, and shall transport them as far as possible to their frontiers.

3. The available forces to be employed against Germany shall be, on the part of France, 1,300,000 men, on the part of Russia, 700,000 or 800,000 men. These forces shall engage to the full with such speed that Germany will have to fight simultaneously on the East and on the West.

4. The General Staffs of the Armies of the two countries shall cooperate with each other at all times to carry out the measures mentioned above

5. France and Russia shall not conclude peace separately.

6. The present Convention shall have the same duration as the Triple Alliance.

Shots at Sarajevo

Austria-Hungary, part of the **Triple Alliance**, controlled an **empire** that extended across much of central Europe. Many of the smaller countries within this empire wanted to become independent, or to join neighbouring, independent countries. Serbia, which occupied an important position in the Balkan Mountains of eastern Europe, was such an independent country. Many Serbs also lived in Bosnia-Herzegovina, which was part of the Austro-Hungarian empire. Serb **nationalists** formed a secret society, known as the Black Hand, to help the Bosnian Serbs to join Serbia. They believed that Serbia would be strengthened – and the empire weakened – if they could trigger a conflict in the region.

Austria-Hungary was eager to keep control of the Balkan region, because it feared that its great rival Russia would gain influence there if Serbia became stronger. Tensions rose in Serbia, but the government of Austria-Hungary remained firm. In late June 1914, Archduke Franz Ferdinand, heir to the Austrian and Hungarian thrones, visited Sarajevo, the capital of Bosnia-Herzegovina. Members of the Black Hand knew of his trip and planned to kill him. Gavrilo Princip, a Serb nationalist, **assassinated** the Archduke and his wife on 28 June 1914.

Archduke Franz Ferdinand and his wife Sofia drive through the streets of Sarajevo. A few minutes later, they would both be killed.

Borijove Jevtic's account of 28 June 1914

Borijove Jevtic was a member of the Black Hand and helped to plan the assassination of Archduke Franz Ferdinand. His account is inaccurate in many ways – there is no evidence, for example, that Archduchess Sofia was pregnant or that Franz Ferdinand was hit in the neck – but it gives a sense of the tense atmosphere on the day.

When Franz Ferdinand's car passed Gabrinovic [a **conspirator**], threw his grenade. It hit the side of the car, but Franz Ferdinand had the presence of mind to throw himself back, and he was uninjured. Several other officers riding in his attendance were injured.

The cars sped to the Town Hall, and the rest of the conspirators did not interfere with them. After the reception in the Town Hall, General Potiorek, the Austrian Commander, pleaded with Franz Ferdinand to leave the city, as it was bubbling over with rebellion. The Archduke was persuaded to drive the shortest way out of the city and to go quickly.

The road was shaped like the letter V, making a sharp turn at the bridge over the River Miljacka. Franz Ferdinand's car could go fast enough until it reached this spot but, here it was forced to slow down for the turn. Here, Princip [another conspirator] had taken his stand.

As the car came alongside him, he stepped forward from the kerb, drew his automatic pistol from his coat and fired two shots. The first struck the wife of the Archduke, the Archduchess Sofia, in the abdomen. She was an expectant mother. She died instantly.

The second bullet struck the Archduke close to the heart.

He uttered only one word, 'Sofia' – a call to his **stricken** wife. Then his head fell back and he collapsed. He died almost instantly.

Europe at war

Many people have described the **assassination** of Archduke Franz Ferdinand as the first shots of World War I. Austria-Hungary blamed Serbia, and sent in troops. All through July 1914, there were frantic attempts to keep the conflict from spreading, but long-standing promises stood in the way. Russia promised to defend Serbia against Austria-Hungary and Germany. Germany declared war on Russia on 1 August 1914 and on France on 3 August.

German troops were sent west, through **neutral** Belgium, towards France. The invasion of Belgium led Great Britain to declare war on Germany. Soon, other countries joined either the **Central Powers** (Germany, Austria-Hungary and their allies) or the **Allied Powers** (Great Britain, France and their allies). Actual fighting began on three major European **fronts**: the western, or Franco-Belgian, front; the eastern, or Russian, front; and the southern, or Serbian, front. With

millions of troops pressed into service, Europe was about to see its biggest war yet. No one could say how it would turn out but, for many people, the actual war came as a relief after years of tense waiting. Now they could channel their energy into something positive – even if it meant risking their lives.

Recruitment posters went up all over Britain persuading men to join the armed forces.

AN APPEAL TO YOU

Sergei N. Kurnakov describes the atmosphere in Russia

The newspaper reporter Sergei N. Kurnakov was in the Russian capital, St Petersburg, when he learned that war had been declared on 1 August 1914. Here, he describes the excitement of the Russian people and their anti-German mood.

There was a crowd outside the newspaper office. Every few minutes a momentous phrase scribbled in charcoal appeared in the window: 'ENGLAND GIVES UP PEACE NEGOTIATIONS. Germany invades Belgium. Mobilization progressing with great enthusiasm.' And at 7:50 p.m.: 'GERMANY DECLARES WAR ON RUSSIA'.

Then the edges of the crowd began breaking off and drifting in one direction, up the Nevsky Prospect. I heard the phrase 'German Embassy' repeated several times. I walked slowly that way.

The crowds were pressing around waiting for something to happen. I was watching a young Russian naval officer being pawed by an over-patriotic group when the steady hammering of axes on metal made me look up at the roof of the German Embassy, which was decorated with huge figures of overfed German warriors holding bloated carthorses.

Several men were hammering at the feet of the **Teutons**. The very first strikes pitched the mob to a frenzy; the heroic figures were hollow!

'Over by Christmas'

Great Britain had fought a war for control of South Africa at the turn of the twentieth century, so its troops had experience of fighting with more modern, powerful weapons. Many soldiers were keen to put this experience to use. They believed that the British, once they were in France, would sweep the Germans back. The **press** echoed this patriotic view, urging young men to **enlist** in the armed forces.

Many British people believed that the war 'would be over by Christmas'. Fired by these words, many young men did enlist, swelling the numbers of British forces by hundreds of thousands. There was a mood of excitement and confidence as the first British soldiers, part of the British Expeditionary Force, arrived in France on 12 August 1914. Some reporters were keen to reflect this confidence, no matter what they actually saw. Others believed that it was important to report the truth as they saw it – that the war would be prolonged and would cost the lives of millions of young soldiers. This approach landed some reporters in trouble with the military authorities.

Philip Gibbs' account
In the early months, the War Office, under the control of Lord Horatio Herbert Kitchener, tried to prevent journalists in France from sending reports back to England. Philip Gibbs, a British reporter, wrote the report on page 15. He was arrested at Le Havre on his way back to the Western **Front**.

Lord Kitchener's war experience in South Africa led to his appointment as British Secretary of State for War in 1914.

Crowds gathered in Fleet Street, London, where most British newspapers had their offices. Everyone was eager for news of the war, but the government was unsure about how much to tell people.

During the early months of the war in 1914 there was a conflict of opinion between the War Office and the Foreign Office regarding news from the Front. The War Office wanted to black out all but the official **communiqués**, and some **innocuous** articles by an official eye-witness (Ernest Swinton). A friend in the War Office warned me that I was in Kitchener's black books, and that orders had been given for my arrest next time I appeared in France.

All was well, until I reached the port of Le Havre. Three officers with the rank of lieutenant, whom afterwards I knew to be Scotland Yard men, came aboard and demanded to see my documents which they took away from me. I was arrested and taken into the presence of General Bruce Williams in command of the base at Le Havre. He put me under house arrest and forbade me all communication with **Fleet Street** or my family. Eventually I succeeded in getting a letter to my boss, explaining my plight. He took instant action and, by the influence of Lord Tyrell at the Foreign Office, I was liberated and allowed to return to England.

The game was up, I thought. I had committed every crime against War Office orders. I should be barred as a war correspondent. So I believed, but in the early part of 1915 I was appointed one of the five men accredited as official war correspondents with the British Armies in the Field.

The German advance

It soon became clear that the war would not be 'over by Christmas'. The British Expeditionary Force, arriving on the continent in the middle to the end of August 1914, soon realized that the Germans were well armed and confident. In fact, the Germans were themselves convinced that the war would end by Christmas – and that they would be celebrating victory. Plus, the Germans had one big advantage – a plan of attack known as the Schlieffen Plan.

The French had prepared for a German attack by building a string of fortresses along the French-German border. But, following the Schlieffen Plan, the Germans avoided these heavily defended French fortresses. They surprised the French by swinging north from Germany, then west through Luxembourg and Belgium, and south into France. They planned to defeat the French before the Russians could play a part in the war. It was up to the French, and their British allies, to stop the Schlieffen Plan in its tracks.

By following the Schlieffen plan, Germany avoided France's defences and rapidly advanced through Belgium.

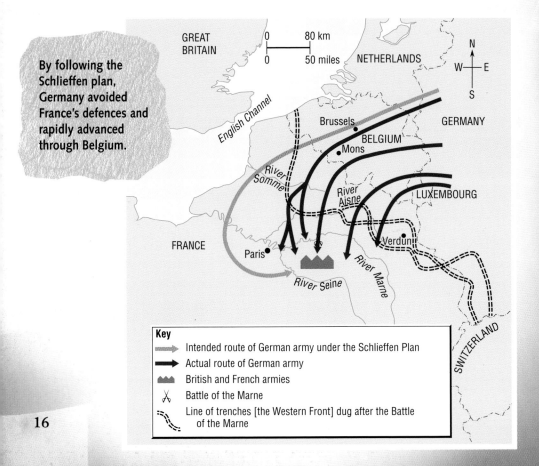

Key

⟶ Intended route of German army under the Schlieffen Plan

➤ Actual route of German army

▲▲▲ British and French armies

✂ Battle of the Marne

⌇ Line of trenches [the Western Front] dug after the Battle of the Marne

Frederic Coleman's experience

Frederic Coleman served with the British Expeditionary Force and was stationed in Messines in south-west Belgium when the Germans advanced in autumn 1914. Here, he describes waiting for the Germans to attack.

The **Hun** was fighting for a pathway to the Channel forts, and for the next three days we had no thought, on our **front**, save that of holding the line against his threatened onslaughts. On the 30th the fighting spread to Messines. For 72 hours from the bursting of that storm of mad fury, we lost all thought of operations on other battlefields. Each hour brought **carnage** and death; each minute was packed full of action.

Messines was becoming a death-trap. I became quite accustomed to hot pieces of **projectile** falling within reach, and black, **pungent** shell-clouds drifting over and around me from the near-by explosion of a **Black Maria**. Experiences one afterwards deems narrow escapes are ridiculously plentiful in a town continually under bombardment. I have ducked quickly round a corner to a doorway grown familiar as a shelter, and left intact but half-an-hour before, to find it choked with debris from the chaotic mass of wood and plaster to which a **howitzer** shell had reduced the interior of the dwelling.

The futility of haste or loitering is demonstrated a hundred times each day. A power far more potent than mere human gunners and the engines of their inventions guides shells. 'Tis just as well to leave it to Him [God]'.

German senior military planner von Schlieffen formed a plan to defeat France before the Russians could prepare for war.

Trench warfare

Along the Western Front, the Germans very nearly succeeded with their plan to defeat France and to force the British to agree upon terms for peace. They came close to capturing Paris and were fighting the French hard near the Belgian border. It was only after a week of fierce fighting, in early September 1914, that the **Allies** were able to halt the German advance. This conflict, known as the Battle of the Marne, marked the start of several years of warfare along the whole Western **Front**.

Held back by the French and British, the Germans dug long trenches to defend their positions. The Allies dug their own trenches, often only metres from the German lines. Neither side could advance quickly, so both sides concentrated on not giving any ground. The pattern was set for the type of fighting for which World War I is remembered. Over the next four years, millions of soldiers would fight in this muddy, grim **stalemate**. The terrible battles of the Western Front – including Ypres and the Somme – were all played out as trench warfare.

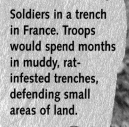

Soldiers in a trench in France. Troops would spend months in muddy, rat-infested trenches, defending small areas of land.

Private Donald Fraser served with the Canadian Expeditionary
Force during World War I. In this excerpt from his journal, he
describes his first experience of life in the trenches. The
soldiers gave nicknames to many of the 'landmarks' in these
enclosed quarters.

September 1915

Our loads were becoming troublesome. We had to rest frequently, but
not for long. Dead Cow Corner was passed and at Beaver Hat we
entered the skeleton remains of a belt of wood. Bullets were cracking
in the trees. Strong Point 11 was soon passed. From here, the trench
began to wind up the base of the Wytschaete Ridge. On our right, the
support line branched off.

A hundred and fifty yards further on, we file into a trench near a
couple of crosses marking the graves of former occupants. We are
now only a few hundred yards away from the enemy so we move
quietly. There is a perfect hiss of bullets overhead and a peculiar hum
from those that **ricochet**. Our own men are firing in return and every
bay gives forth a crack, crack. It is the custom as soon as darkness
sets in for both sides to keep up a more or less continuous fire at
each other's trenches, to keep one another from attacking and also, to
keep patrols from **No Man's Land**. It also shows that one is awake
and there is not the same chance of being taken by surprise. The
tendency, when firing in the dark, is to fire high, with the result that
most of the bullets go flying over the trenches, maybe to find a victim
2000 yards behind; many men get killed in this fashion.

The Eastern Front

Although the most destructive combat in World War I took place along the Western **Front** (Belgium and France), central and eastern Europe also saw some terrible fighting. After all, the war itself had erupted when Austria-Hungary had decided to crush Serbia's move to become more powerful. Italy, which had remained **neutral** for a year, joined the **Allied Powers** in 1915, but that same year saw Turkey (then known as the Ottoman Empire) entering the war on the side of the **Central Powers**.

The stage was set for fierce fighting to control the Balkan Region, central Europe and the eastern Mediterranean. Russia was a key Allied player along this Eastern Front. Its huge army pierced into Austrian and Hungarian territory, but its troops were badly supplied and unable to hold their gains. However, the troubles were not all on Russia's side. Austria-Hungary relied on troops from the many small nations that made up its **Empire**. Many of these soldiers had no real loyalty to Austria-Hungary – or to their fellow troops from other nations. The end result was confusion and chaos amid the bloodshed.

The Eastern Front involved fighting between Central Powers Germany and Austria-Hungary and, one of the Allied powers, Russia.

Bernard Pares's account

The fortress-town of Przemysl, in eastern Hungary, was one of the most heavily defended places in Europe. Bernard Pares's account of its capture by the Russians, on 22 March 1915, shows how rivalries among its defenders led to its downfall.

Even a few days before, quite well-informed people had no idea that the end was coming so soon. The town was a first-class fortress, whose development had been an object of special concern to the late Archduke Franz Ferdinand. It was generally understood that Przemysl was **garrisoned** by about 50,000 men. The stores were said to be enough for a **siege** of three years. The circle of the forts was so extended as to make operations easy against any but the largest **blockading** force; and the **aerodrome**, which was well covered, gave communication with the outside world.

For weeks past the fortress had kept up a terrific fire which was greater than any experienced elsewhere from Austrian artillery. Thousands of shells yielded only tens of wounded, and it would seem that the Austrians could have had no other object than to get rid of their **ammunition**.

Now followed extraordinary scenes. Austrian soldiers were seen fighting each other, while the Russians looked on. Amid the chaos a small group of staff officers appeared, casually enough, with a white flag, and announced surrender.

The greatest surprise of all was the strength of the **garrison**, which numbered not 50,000 but 130,000. The troops, instead of being all Hungarians, were of various Austrian nationalities; and there is good reason to think that the conditions of defence led to feuds, brawls and, in the end, open disobedience of orders.

Gallipoli

In April 1915, the **Allied Powers** launched an attack on the Gallipoli peninsula, which guards the narrow passage of water leading to Istanbul and the Black Sea (see map on page 20). This attack was meant to damage Turkish defences and to open a supply route to Russia, which was one of the Allies. Instead, a combination of poor Allied leadership and stiff Turkish defence turned the action into a long, deadly struggle. At one point, in August 1915, some 4000 Allied soldiers died while trying to gain just 400 metres of ground. Many of the Allied soldiers were part of the Australian–New Zealand Army Corps (ANZAC), which fought alongside the British.

Both sides suffered terrible casualties by the time the Allies withdrew in January 1916 – roughly 250,000 on the Allied side alone. Despite the fierce fighting, the battle for Gallipoli ended with no clear victory for either side. It did, however, weaken the Turks and open the way for future British successes in the eastern Mediterranean region.

Allied soldiers land on the narrow beaches of the Gallipoli peninsula. As they climbed the steep cliffs, many were men gunned down by enemy machine-guns perched on top.

Lance-Corporal Samuel Weingott's diary

Lance-Corporal Samuel Weingott of Australia was part of the ANZAC force that fought in Gallipoli in 1915 and 1916. These are his last diary entries – he died in action on 5 June 1915.

Sunday 23rd May 1915

Working night and day. Am feeling very fatigued. Had narrow escape of being shot clean through the head, but bullet strikes a sandbag immediately in front of me. Turks rather quiet.

Monday 24th May

Armistice of seven hours granted to bury the dead. 400 dead Turks found in front of 1st Battalion lines. Also 185 Rifles. Rain continues throughout the day. 80 Turks found dead in one small trench.

Tuesday 25th May

Austrian submarine sinks the *Triumph* 11,000 tons in sixteen minutes in sight of the Australian troops. 785 souls on board. 150 drowned. I read the burial service. Submarine captured during the night. Enemy rather quiet.

Wednesday 26th May

Reinforcements arrive. Still working night and day; been on for the last five days without a rest. Aeroplane drops two bombs into the enemy's trenches 30 yards from us. Enemy keep us very busy. **Snipers** serving well.

Saturday 29th May

Tremendous **bombardment** by the enemy guns commencing at 3 a.m. They fire at point blank, doing great damage to our trenches. One shell burst in my face and, although unwounded, was knocked out for a few minutes. My rifle was twisted beyond recognition.

Thursday 3rd June

Warship fires incessantly at Turkish transports laden with **ammunition** and foodstuffs from Constantinople, and blow them to pieces. Six hundred mules reported to have been killed. Enemy rather quiet owing to supposed shortage of ammunition.

Battles in the air

The aeroplane had been invented just over a decade before World War I began. Few people in 1914 had seen a plane, let alone flown in one. The military leaders on both sides soon found ways to put the new invention to use. They used planes for **reconnaissance**, for carrying urgent messages and even for bombing raids (although the raids were limited and could never destroy long trenches). Nothing captured the public imagination as much as the **aerial** battles, or 'dogfights', between fighter aircraft known as 'scouts'.

The daring pilots who battled each other in the skies were popular heroes. Newspapers carried accounts of each pilot's 'kill', and the most successful fighter pilots were treated like pop stars are treated today. Each country had its special heroes, but no fighter pilot gained as much respect and awe as Manfred von Richthofen of Germany. He was nicknamed the 'Red Baron', because he painted his plane bright red to taunt the enemy. He shot down 80 **Allied** aircraft in under three years. In 1916, the Red Baron was shot down and killed in France.

The 'Red Baron's account of his success
The 'Red Baron' wrote about his successes, in order to boost German **morale**. On page 25, he describes his first victim, a British plane shot down on 17 September 1915.

Fighter planes battle among the clouds in 'dogfights'.

Slowly, we approached the hostile **squadron**. It could not escape us. We had intercepted it, for we were between the **Front** and our opponents. If they wished to go back, they had to pass us. We counted the hostile machines. They were seven in number. We were only five. All the Englishmen flew large bomb-carrying two-seaters.

Manfred von Richthofen, known as the 'Red Baron' shot down 80 Allied planes in his red-painted fighter aircraft.

In a few seconds, the dance would begin. The Englishman nearest to me was travelling in a large plane painted with dark colours. I did not reflect very long, but took my aim and shot. He also fired and so did I, and both of us missed our aim. A struggle began, and the great point for me was to get to the rear of the pilot, because I could only shoot forward with my gun. He was differently placed, because his machine gun was movable. It could fire in all directions.

Apparently, he was no beginner, for he knew exactly that his last hour had arrived at the moment when I got at the back of him. My Englishman twisted and turned, going criss-cross. At last, a favourable moment arrived. My opponent had apparently lost sight of me. Instead of twisting and turning, he flew straight along. In a fraction of a second, I was at his back with my excellent machine. I gave a short series of shots with my machine gun. Suddenly, I nearly yelled with joy, because the propeller of the enemy machine had stopped turning. I had shot his engine to pieces; the enemy was forced to land, because it was impossible for him to reach his own lines.

U-boats

The **Central Powers** knew that they were at a disadvantage when it came to control of the seas. Great Britain, one of the leading **Allied Powers**, had a reputation for naval success going back more than two centuries. Although the Germans, in particular, had built up their fleet in the pre-war years, their ships could not match the British battleships, cruisers and destroyers. The British used their ships to **blockade** the German coast, cutting off the German fleet and the supply of important goods to Germany.

Germany decided to build a fleet of submarines, which they called U-boats. Using skill and cunning, U-boat captains began sinking Allied ships by suddenly surfacing and opening fire with cannons. They saved their precious torpedoes for attacks on warships. What started as a method of defence turned to attack, as U-boats nearly turned the tables on the British. Soon, it was Great Britain that faced a blockade, as German submarines threatened any ship travelling to or from British ports.

A German U-boat attacks a British merchant ship. By stopping the supply of essential goods, Germany tried to starve Britain into defeat.

MC DOWELL

Adolf K.G.E. von Spiegel describes a torpedo attack

Adolf K.G.E. von Spiegel was captain of the German U-Boat 202, patrolling the Atlantic. Here, he describes a torpedo attack on a British ship in April 1916.

The steamer appeared to be close to us, and looked enormous. I saw the captain walking on his **bridge**, a small whistle in his mouth. I saw the crew cleaning the deck forward, and I saw, with surprise and a slight shudder, long rows of wooden partitions right along the decks, from which gleamed the shining black and brown backs of horses.

'Oh, heavens, horses! What a pity, those lovely beasts!'

'But it cannot be helped,' I went on thinking. 'War is war, and every horse the fewer on the Western front is a reduction of England's fighting power.'

There were only a few more degrees to go before the steamer would be on the correct **bearing**.

'Stand by for firing a torpedo!' I called down to the control room. Everyone held his breath.

'FIRE!'

A slight tremor went through the boat – the torpedo had gone.

The death-bringing shot was a true one, and the torpedo ran towards the doomed ship at high speed. I could follow its course exactly by the light streak of bubbles which was left in its wake. I saw that the bubble-track of the torpedo had been discovered on the bridge of the steamer, as frightened arms pointed towards the water and the captain put his hands in front of his eyes and waited. Then a frightful explosion followed, and we were all thrown against one other. and then, huge and majestic, a column of water 200 metres high and 50 metres broad, terrible in its beauty and power, shot up to the heavens.

The Irish uprising

The same **nationalist** feelings that drove the Serbs and other European nations to want independence around the turn of the twentieth century also simmered in Ireland. At the start of World War I, Great Britain suspended a **bill** that would have given Ireland **Home Rule**. This led James Connolly and other leading **nationalists** to set up a Citizen Army to fight for Irish independence.

In early 1916, the Citizen Army joined forces with two other nationalist groups, the Irish Volunteers and Sinn Fein, to begin a full-scale rebellion against British rule. The Irish uprising began on 24 April 1916 (Easter Monday), when about 2000 men, led by Patrick Pearse, seized control of Dublin's general post office and other points in the city. The leaders of the rebellion then proclaimed the independence of Ireland, and announced the establishment of a provisional (temporary) government of the Irish Republic.

The rebels' success did not last. The British fought back, forcing Pearse and his followers to surrender. The leaders were tried under British law. Fifteen (including Pearse and Connolly) were executed. The rebellion lasted only five days, but it marked the first step towards Irish independence five years later. Meanwhile, thousands of other Irishmen had joined British forces on the continent.

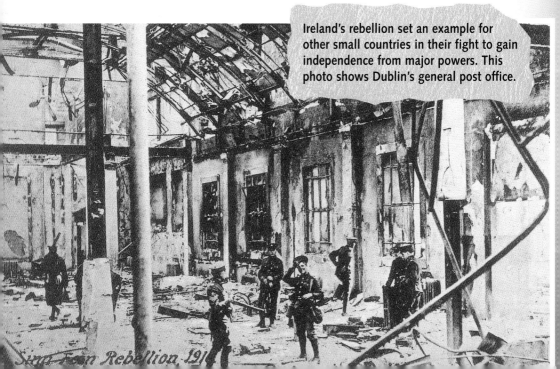

Ireland's rebellion set an example for other small countries in their fight to gain independence from major powers. This photo shows Dublin's general post office.

James Stephens's diary

The author James Stephens took part in the Easter Uprising of 1916. This passage comes from a diary he kept to record the events of that week.

Wednesday

It was three o'clock before I got to sleep last night, and during the hours machine guns and rifle firing had been continuous. This morning, the sun is shining brilliantly, and the movement in the streets possesses more energy than it has done. The movement ends always in a knot of people, and folk go from group to group vainly seeking information, and quite content if the rumour they presently gather differs even a little from the one they have just communicated. The first statement I heard was that the Green [St Stephen's Green, a Dublin park] had been taken by British soldiers; the second, that it had been re-taken; the third, that it had not been taken at all. The facts at last emerged that the Green had not been occupied by the soldiers, but that the **volunteers** had retreated from it into a house which commanded it. This was found to be the College of Surgeons, and from the windows and roof of this College they were **sniping**. A machine gun was mounted on the roof; other machine guns, however, opposed them from the roofs of the Shelbourne Hotel, the United Service Club and the Alexandra Club. Thus, a triangular duel opened between these positions across the trees of the Park. Through the railings of the Green, some rifles and **bandoliers** could be seen lying on the ground, as also the deserted trenches and snipers' holes. Small boys bolted in to see these sights. Small boys do not believe that people will really kill them, but small boys were killed.

The Battle of Jutland

For centuries, Britain's history has been linked to naval power. The Royal Navy has been both a defence against invasion and a way of gaining power for Britain. During World War I, the **Central Powers** – and Germany in particular – needed to weaken British naval strength. German U-boats (see pages 26–27) did some of this job, destroying British warships and cargo ships with ease. They also opened the sea passage for Germany's fleet, which had been hemmed in by a British **blockade**.

By mid-1916, Germany felt ready to fight the Royal Navy head-on. It was only a matter of time before there would be a showdown between these two great naval powers. It came over a two-day period (31 May–1 June 1916) in the Battle of Jutland, just off the Danish coast. The immediate outcome seemed indecisive – and the British even lost more men and ships than the Germans – but the battle weakened the German navy so that it could never again threaten British control of the North Sea and English Channel.

Ernest Francis's experience

Ernest Francis served as an officer on the British battle-cruiser *Queen Mary* during the Battle of Jutland. He was in charge of one of the gun **turrets**. On page 31, he describes how the crew continued to battle on, even after the ship had been hit by a deadly blow.

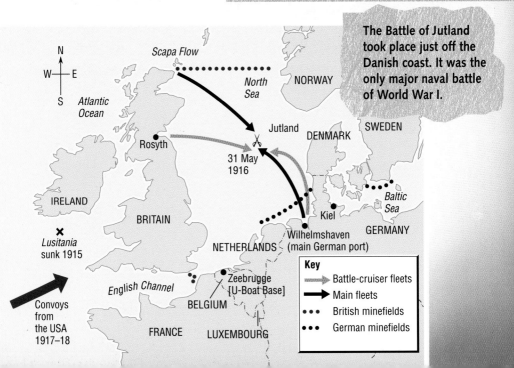

The Battle of Jutland took place just off the Danish coast. It was the only major naval battle of World War I.

N
W–E
S

Atlantic
Ocean

Scapa Flow

North
Sea

NORWAY

Jutland
DENMARK

SWEDEN

Rosyth

31 May
1916

IRELAND

BRITAIN

Baltic
Sea

Kiel

✕
Lusitania
sunk 1915

NETHERLANDS

Wilhelmshaven
(main German port)

GERMANY

Convoys
from
the USA
1917–18

English Channel

BELGIUM

Zeebrugge
[U-Boat Base]

FRANCE   LUXEMBOURG

Key
- ⇒ Battle-cruiser fleets
- → Main fleets
- ••• British minefields
- ••• German minefields

A ship is under fire in the Battle of Jutland. This great naval battle weakened the German navy.

Another shock was felt but it did not affect the turret, so no notice was taken. Then one of the men reported to Lieutenant Ewert that the third German ship of the line was dropping out. First blood to the *Queen Mary*. The shout they gave was good to hear. I could not resist giving a quick look at her, at their request, and I found that the third ship of the line was going down by the **bows**.

I looked again and saw that the third ship of the line was gone. I took another look through my telescope and there was quite a fair distance between the second ship and what I believed was the fourth ship, due I think to the third ship going under. Flames were belching from what I took to be the fourth ship of the line, then came the big explosion which shook us a bit. Immediately after that came, what I term, the big smash, and I was dangling in the air on a **bowline**, which saved me from being thrown down on the floor of the turret.

Everything in the ship went as quiet as a church. The floor of the turret was bulged up and the guns were absolutely useless. One man turned to me and said, 'What do you think has happened?'

Total war

One of the features that distinguished World War I from previous conflicts was its huge scale, with millions of men fighting for both the **Allied Powers** and the **Central Powers**. Coupled with this was a new warfare **strategy**, which military experts now describe as 'total war'. For the first time in history, fighting went beyond the battlefield and deliberately threatened **civilians**.

Both sides in World War I targeted non-military areas, such as major cities and ports. Part of the reason for this strategy was to cripple factories that might be producing war materials, such as guns, hand grenades and shells. Just as importantly, these attacks were meant to scare ordinary people, destroying their will to fight. Raids by German zeppelins (a type of **airship**) and aircraft on eastern England and London killed many people.

German air raids using these vast airships terrified the people of eastern England.

Michael MacDonagh's account
British artillery fought hard to bring down invading zeppelins, often succeeding with spectacular results. Michael MacDonagh, a journalist, witnessed the destruction of German Zeppelin L31 on 1 October 1916. His account is on page 33.

I saw last night what is probably the most terrible spectacle associated with the war which London is likely to provide – the bringing down of a raiding Zeppelin.

I was late at the office and, leaving it just before midnight, I was crossing to Blackfriars Bridge to get a tramcar home, when my attention was attracted by frenzied cries of 'Oh! Oh! She's hit!' from some travellers who were standing in the middle of the road gazing at the sky in a northern direction. Looking up I saw high in the sky a concentrated blaze of searchlights and, in its centre, a bright glow which rapidly spread into the outline of a blazing airship. Then the searchlights were turned off and the Zeppelin drifted nose down in the darkened sky, a gigantic pyramid of flames, red and orange, like a ruined star falling slowly to earth. Its glare lit up the streets and gave a bright tint even to the waters of the Thames.

The spectacle lasted two or three minutes. It was so horribly fascinating that I felt spellbound – almost suffocated with emotion, ready to laugh or cry. When, at last, the doomed airship vanished from sight there arose a shout the like of which I never heard in London before – a hoarse shout of mixed cursing, triumph and joy; a swelling shout that appeared to be rising from all parts of the city, ever increasing in force and intensity.

The USA enters the war

The USA favoured the **Allied Powers**, but they did not enter World War I immediately. Many Americans saw it as a 'European war', which did not affect their lives. Also, a great number of Americans were the children or grandchildren of German **immigrants**, and they had little desire to fight against the 'mother country'. After the Germans sank a British passenger ship, the *Lusitania*, in May 1915, killing more than 100 US citizens, many Americans favoured entering the war, but the '**isolationist**' mood was stronger. As the son of a church minister, US president Woodrow Wilson had his own reasons to avoid bloodshed. He tried to act as a peacemaker in the first two years of the war, proposing peace plans to both sides in the conflict.

Wilson changed his attitude in early 1917, when the German government decided to mount an all-out submarine assault on Britain. The USA strongly opposed this, and even viewed it as a threat to its own vessels. On 6 April 1917, the USA declared war on Germany, an act that helped to tip the balance in favour of the Allies.

General John Pershing, in the centre, commander of US troops in Europe, inspects a parade of soldiers in France.

Sherwood Eddy's battle experience

Sherwood Eddy, an American author, travelled to Europe with the first US soldiers to fight in World War I. Here, he describes the sights and sounds of the battlefield to US readers who might have been unfamiliar with the horrors of the war.

High above, we hear the piercing shriek of the shells speeding to their fatal mark and, below, the crash of the exploding shells of the enemy. Gun after gun now joins the great chorus. The whole horizon is lit up and aflame. The sky shakes and reflects the flash of the great guns. Flares and **Verey** lights of greenish yellow and white turn the night into ghastly day, and like the vivid flames of a raging fire light up the battlefield, while the rifles crackle in the glare.

Here a parachute-light like a great star hangs suspended almost motionless above us, lighting up the whole battlefield, and now a burning farmhouse or exploding ammunition dump illuminates the sky as from some vast subterranean (underground) furnace flung open upon the heavens. All the long sullen night the earth is rocked by slow intermittent rumbling, till with the silent dawn the birds wake and the war-giants sink for a few hours in troubled sleep.

American soldiers on their way to the battlefields of Europe. The Allies gained a great advantage when America entered the war in April 1917.

Gas attacks

Poisonous gases had been known about for a long time before 1914, but military officers had been reluctant to use this terrible weapon. That attitude changed during World War I. In the first month of the war, the French army used tear gas against the Germans. In 1915, the Germans began to release chlorine gas from containers on the battlefield. This gas destroyed the **respiratory** organs of its victims, leading to a slow death by asphyxiation (suffocation).

After the first German chlorine gas attacks, **Allied** troops began using masks of cotton pads that had been soaked in urine. They found that the ammonia in the urine counteracted the poison. It was

not until July 1915 that soldiers were given efficient gas masks and anti-asphyxiation **respirators**, or 'gas masks'. However, even these were sometimes not enough to combat this deadly weapon that killed so slowly.

After World War I, most countries condemned the use of poison gas, and resolved never to use it again in warfare.

Gas masks were issued to soldiers serving in the trenches, in order to combat deadly gas attacks.

William Pressey, a British soldier, was gassed on 7 June 1917 at Messines Ridge in south-west Belgium.
He survived the attack and, later, wrote about the experience of being gassed.

I was awakened by a terrific crash. The roof came down on my chest and legs, and I couldn't move anything but my head. I found I could hardly breathe. Then I heard voices. Other men with gas helmets on were lifting timber off me and one was forcing a gas helmet on me.

I was put into an ambulance and taken to the base, where we were placed on the stretchers side by side on the floor of a large tent. I suppose I resembled a kind of fish, with my mouth open gasping for air. It seemed as if my lungs were gradually shutting up and my heart pounded away in my ears like the beat of a drum. On looking at the chap next to me I felt sick, for green stuff was oozing from the side of his mouth.

To get air in my lungs was real agony. I dozed off for short periods, but seemed to wake in a sort of panic. To ease the pain in my chest, I may subconsciously have stopped breathing, until the pounding of my heart woke me up. I was always surprised when I found myself awake, for I felt sure that I would die in my sleep.

Turmoil in Russia

At the start of World War I, Russia was ruled by Tsar Nicholas II. The tsar had enormous power, but did not seem to understand the problems of his country. A very few rich people controlled most of Russia's land and business, while most Russians were peasants and factory workers. They worked hard, but saw little chance to improve their condition. The strain of scraping out a living was made worse by the sacrifices needed for the war effort. By early 1917, the country was ready for some sort of powerful protest.

The Russian **Revolution** of February 1917 dismissed the tsarist government. The new provisional (temporary) government tried to continue the war effort, although most Russians demanded immediate changes to their lives. In October 1917, a second revolution erupted in Russia. Its leader was a **communist** revolutionary named Vladimir Lenin. The new communist government swept to power with the slogan 'Peace, Land and Bread', and their first step was to end Russian involvement in World War I.

The people of Russia wanted immediate change, and armed revolutionaries succeeded in overthrowing the government.

John Reed's account

John Reed was a US journalist who became friendly with Vladimir Lenin. Here, he describes the dramatic events of 25 October 1917. Communist Red Guards and pro-revolutionary soldiers swept into the Winter Palace (the seat of the tsarist and, later, provisional governments) in the Russian capital, St Petersburg.

Carried along by the eager wave of men, we were swept into the right-hand entrance, opening into the cellar of the east wing, from which issued a maze of corridors and staircases. A number of huge packing cases stood about, and upon these the Red Guards and soldiers fell furiously, battering them open with the butts of their rifles, and pulling out carpets, curtains, linen, porcelain, plates, glassware.

The **looting** was just beginning when somebody cried 'Comrades! Don't take anything. This is the Property of the People!' Immediately 20 voices were crying. 'Stop! Put everything back! Don't take anything! Property of the People!' Roughly and hastily, items were crammed back in their cases, and self-appointed sentinels stood guard. Through corridors and up staircases the cry could be heard growing fainter and fainter in the distance, 'Revolutionary discipline! Property of the People.'

We crossed back over to the west wing. 'Clear the Palace!' bawled a Red Guard, sticking his head through an inner door. 'Come, comrades, let's show that we're not thieves and bandits. Everybody out of the Palace except the **Commissars**, until we get sentinels posted.'

The wider conflict

World War I was a world conflict, involving some major fighting outside Europe. The main land fighting was in Africa, where **Allied** forces (mainly British and French) struggled to gain control of German **colonies**. Most of Germany's possessions in West Africa fell to the Allies early on, but East Africa was different. The advantage swayed back and forth, and there was still fighting going on here at the end of the war.

Another important World War I battleground was the Middle East near the eastern Mediterranean. There, the Allies joined forces with local Arab fighters in order to combat the Turkish rulers of the region, who were part of the **Central Powers**. The Allies were determined to gain control of the eastern Mediterranean because it was such an important region. Vital trade routes, especially through the Suez Canal (connecting the Mediterranean and Red seas) passed through this area. The first Allied attempt to gain control, in Gallipoli (see pages 22–23), was not a success. Later in the war, the Allies concentrated their efforts in Arabia and other lands controlled by the Turks.

One of the most famous British soldiers in the region was Colonel T. E. Lawrence, known as 'Lawrence of Arabia'. He was sent to the Middle East in 1916 to help the Arabs against the Turks. For two years, Lawrence and his band of Arab fighters attacked Turkish positions, cut off communications, destroyed railways and supported the British army in the military advance north to Damascus (see map on page 20).

T. E. Lawrence's letter

In this extract from a letter written to a close friend, T. E. Lawrence describes a raid against the Turkish-controlled Hejaz Railway, near Harret Ammar in Arabia (known as Jordan today). The letter is dated 24 September 1917, two days after the raid took place.

The last stunt was the hold-up of a train. It had two engines, and we destroyed one with an electric mine. This rather jumbled up the trucks, which were full of Turks shooting at us.

We had a **Lewis**, and flung bullets through the sides. So they hopped out and took cover behind the **embankment**, and shot at us between the wheels, at 50 yards. Then we tried a **Stokes gun**, and two beautiful shots dropped right in the middle of them. They couldn't stand that (twelve died on the spot), and bolted away to the east across a 100-yard belt of open sand into some bushes. Unfortunately for them, the Lewis covered the open stretch.

The whole job took ten minutes, and they lost 70 killed, 30 wounded, 80 prisoners and about 25 got away. Of my 100 **Howeitat** and two British officers, there was one Arab killed and four Arabs wounded.

The Turks then nearly cut us off as we **looted** the train, and I lost some baggage, and nearly myself. My loot is a superfine red prayer-rug.

Colonel T. E. Lawrence, known as Lawrence of Arabia, led the Arabs in a number of daring attacks on the Turks.

War poetry

Few people could make sense of a war that was so vicious and wide-ranging, cutting down millions of men in their youth. Soldiers, in their letters home, tried to give an idea of life in the trenches, but many could not describe their true feelings of horror and sadness. Others were simply overwhelmed by a powerful type of depression, known as **shell shock**.

Artists and writers felt it was a duty to make some sort of sense of the war. War artists sketched and painted pictures of battlefields and soldiers, but it was writing – especially poetry – that captured the essence of World War I. The German writer Erich Maria Remarque described the tenderness and emotions of ordinary soldiers in his novel *All Quiet on the Western Front*. Ernest Hemingway gave an American's view of the fighting in his novel *A Farewell to Arms*. The works of Britain's 'war poets', notably Wilfred Owen, Siegfried Sassoon and Robert Graves, also provide a lasting testament to the 'Great War'.

Siegfried Sassoon's writings tell of the horror and sadness of World War I.

A poem by Siegfried Sassoon

Siegfried Sassoon served as an officer in the British Army during World War I. He was saddened by the idea that the promise of youth was snuffed out by senseless death. This theme dominated Sassoon's writings – both novels and poems – until his death in 1967.

'Aftermath' (1920)

Have you forgotten yet?...
For the world's events have rumbled on since those **gagged** days,
Like traffic checked while at the crossing of city-ways:
And the haunted gap in your mind has filled with thoughts that flow
Like clouds in the lit heaven of life; and you're a man **reprieved** to go,
Taking your peaceful share of Time, with joy to spare.
But the past is just the same-and War's a bloody game...
Have you forgotten yet?...
Look down, and swear by the slain of the War that you'll never forget.
Do you remember the dark months you held the sector at Mametz-
The nights you watched and wired and dug and piled sandbags on
parapets?
Do you remember the rats; and the stench
Of corpses rotting in front of the front-line trench -
And dawn coming, dirty-white, and chill with a hopeless rain?
Do you ever stop and ask, 'Is it all going to happen again?'
Do you remember that hour of **din** before the attack -
And the anger, the blind compassion that seized and shook you then
As you peered at the doomed and **haggard** faces of your men?
Do you remember the stretcher-cases lurching back
With dying eyes and lolling heads-those ashen-grey
Masks of the lads who once were keen and kind and **gay**?

Have you forgotten yet?...
Look up, and swear by the green of the spring that you'll never forget.

Turning the tide

By the middle of 1918, it became clear that the **Allied Powers** were gaining the advantage in the war. Although Russia played no part in the Allied efforts after its **revolution** (see pages 38–39), US involvement helped to tip the balance. In August 1918, British troops began a series of advances against German positions in northern France. Teaming up with the French, they broke through the German lines at various points across northern France in early September. These victories set the Germans on retreat in northern France. At the same time, US forces pushed through eastern France towards Germany.

Signs were just as hopeful in eastern Europe. A combined Allied force swept the Austrians out of Serbia and much of the Balkans, while Italian troops began to drive the Austrians north. The two main **Central Powers**, Austria-Hungary and Germany, were beginning to feel under pressure.

In the autumn of 1918, British and French troops advanced steadily against German positions in northern France.

Robert Lindsay Mackay's journal

Robert Lindsay Mackay was an officer with the Argyll and Sutherland Highlanders from 1915 until the end of the war. This journal entry reflects the confident mood of the soldiers in autumn 1918, as they made more and more advances against the retreating Germans in northern France.

1 October 1918

At 6 p.m., I went along to fix up food, and then opened a new headquarters in the old **front** line at 7 p.m. Busy night again. Messages coming and going. Very dark. No moon. No sleep. Our patrols worked during the night. It was apparent in many ways that the **Hun** meant to hold his third line but our early move, where we broke in and rolled up his **flanks**, upset him. Nairn's work was '**A.L.**'. We got twelve prisoners, seven machine guns, and killed 27 **Boches**. By 8 a.m. on 2 October patrols were working into Vendin. Lord, it was grand!

Much **sniping**. Capt. Billy Irvine on the right simply in his element. People further to the right somewhat slow – opposition from a **switch line** held them up slightly. Battalion headquarters to Bois de Quatorze at 11 a.m. Relieved at night by Royal Scots. Our total casualties five killed and about 20 wounded.

Back to Loos on 3–4 October. Grand feed on arrival at old **dressing station**. Bed at 1 a.m. on 4th. Slept like a log for eight hours. **Bumph** all day.

6th. Boche asked for **armistice**. Hurrah! Hope we don't give it until we reach the Rhine.

The armistice

By early autumn 1918, the steady **Allied** pressure on the Western and Eastern **Fronts** weakened the **Central Powers**. Having been defeated in the Balkans, the Austrians suffered a terrible defeat in northern Italy at the Battle of Vittorio Veneto (24 October–4 November 1918). The Allies took several hundred thousand Austrian prisoners, and the rest of the Austrian army fled to Austria. Seeing defeat, the Austrian government reached an **armistice** with the Allies the day before the Battle of Vittorio Veneto ended.

The Germans, meanwhile, had reached the same point. German representatives met with the Allies from late October onwards. Each day brought news of further Allied advances. Finally, at 5 a.m. on 11 November 1918, an armistice was signed between Germany and the Allies. Under the terms of the armistice, fighting ended at 11 a.m. that same day. The war had ended. The news spread quickly around Europe and the world, and celebrations began immediately.

A group of soldiers celebrate in London on Armistice Day – after four long years, World War I was finally over.

F.A. Voigt's memories

F.A. Voigt, a US soldier, recalled the atmosphere on the front when news of the armistice spread among the soldiers. Although they had been expecting this news, the soldiers erupted in a joyful celebration, as if they could not believe their ears.

Darkness came on and we retired to our tents. I gradually became aware of a faint noise, so faint that I hardly knew whether it was real or not. Then one of us said: 'What's that funny noise?' There it was again, a low, hollow sound like that of a distant sea. It grew louder and then ceased. Then it grew louder and still louder. Suddenly we realized what it was – it was the sound of cheering. It came nearer and nearer, gathering speed, and then burst over our camp.

Everybody went mad. The men rushed out of the tents and shouted: 'It's over – it's over – it's over!' I could hear one shrill voice screaming wildly: 'No more bombs – no more shells – no more misery'. The deafening noise from innumerable throats was topped by the piercing blasts of whistles and the howling of cat calls. A huge bonfire was lit in the camp and sheets of flame shot skyward. The brilliant stars of signal-rockets rose and fell in tall arcs, and lit up all the neighbourhood. The Sergeant Major blew his whistle with the intention of restoring order. He was answered by dismissive hoots and yells. He gave up the attempt. An anti-aircraft unit opened fire with blank charges. Aeroplanes flew overhead with all lights on.

A lasting peace?

The **armistice** ended the fighting, but there was still the matter of deciding how peace could be secured. US president Woodrow Wilson proposed forming a **League of Nations** to act as a worldwide 'policeman' to prevent local conflicts becoming major wars. Other **Allied Powers** believed that the **Central Powers** – especially Germany – should be made to pay for the damage they caused by starting the war.

These two conflicting aims created a confused mood as representatives met to discuss a **treaty**. They gathered in the French town of Versailles, on 18 January 1919. After five months of negotiations, the representatives signed what is now known as the Treaty of Versailles, on 28 June 1919. It echoed the conflicting aims of the representatives who had taken part. On the one hand, the treaty established a League of Nations. On the other hand, Germany and Austria lost some of their territory, and were forced to pay large **reparations**. Some historians say that these harsh penalties against Germany led to the rise of Adolf Hitler – and the next world war only 20 years later.

British prime minister David Lloyd George, French premier Georges Clemenceau and US president Woodrow Wilson (left to right) at the Versailles peace conference.

The memoirs of Sir Harold Nicolson

Sir Harold Nicolson was part of the British **delegation** to the Treaty of Versailles. The extract from his memoirs offers a first-hand account of the drama of this important event in world history.

People step over the elegant benches to talk to friends. Meanwhile, the representatives arrive in little bunches and push up the central aisle slowly. US President Woodrow Wilson and British Prime Minister David Lloyd George are among the last. They take their seats at the central table. The table is, at last, full. French Premier Georges Clemenceau glances to right and left. People sit down but continue chattering. Clemenceau makes a sign to the **ushers**. They say 'Ssh! Ssh! Ssh' People cease chattering, and there is only the sound of occasional coughing and the dry rustle of programmes. There is then an absolute hush, followed by a sharp military order. The Gardes Republicaines [French military guards] at the doorway flash their swords into their **scabbards** with a loud click. 'Faites entrer les Allemends' ['Let the Germans enter'], says Clemenceau in the ensuing silence.

Through the door at the end appear two **hussars**. After them come four officers of France, Great Britain, America and Italy. And then, isolated and pitiable, come the two German delegates, Dr Muller, Dr Bell. The silence is terrifying. Their feet on the wooden floor echo hollow and duplicate. They keep their eyes fixed away from those two thousand staring eyes, fixed upon the ceiling. They are deathly pale. They do not appear as representatives of brutal militarism. It is almost painful.

Sir Harold Nicolson was present at the peace conference, where the Treaty of Versailles was signed.

What have we learnt from World War I?

The wide ranging effects of World War I were devastating, with millions of men dead and countries facing severe hardship after such a long, costly conflict. Moreover, the harsh terms the peace treaty inflicted on Germany contributed to the rise of Adolf Hitler and a second world war 20 years later. Since then world leaders have become more aware of political situations that may trigger major conflicts, and are determined to resolve disputes before they spread into global wars.

Determined to avoid another devastating world war, leaders set up the United Nations to resolve conflicts around the globe. The UN peacekeeping force enters war zones to help put a stop to fighting.

We can see the effects of World War I all around us. Nearly every community in Britain – and in France and Belgium – has a war memorial dedicated to the men who died during the war. Each year, on the Sunday nearest to 11 November (the date of the main **armistice**), the Queen and senior politicians make their way solemnly to the Whitehall Cenotaph, the great War Memorial in London. There, they lay wreaths to display the nation's gratitude for the great sacrifices made by the fallen soldiers of World War I. Old soldiers and their families also pay their respects to those who died in the 'Great War'.

Queen Elizabeth II's speech
Queen Elizabeth II visited Paris on 11 November 1998, to mark the 80th anniversary of the end of World War I. The passage on page 51 is from her official speech, which she delivered in French and English.

A remembrance ceremony at the Menin Gate in Ypres, Belgium. A memorial lists the names of more than 55,000 British soldiers, whose bodies were never recovered from the nearby battlefield.

Exactly 80 years ago today, the guns fell silent in Europe after four long, terrible years of war. Some eight million lives had been lost. On one summer's day in Northern France in 1916, more than 56,000 young British soldiers were killed or wounded on the Somme. In one battle, Verdun, more than a quarter of a million French and German soldiers paid 'the Price of Glory'.

Last Sunday, on Remembrance Sunday, as I have done virtually every year of my reign, I laid a wreath at the Cenotaph in London, in solemn memory of all those who have died in war. This morning, I had the privilege of participating with President Chirac in the ceremony at the Tomb of the Unknown Soldier at the Arc de Triomphe, and then honouring the memory of Georges Clemençeau at his memorial.

This afternoon, I will join President McAleese of Ireland on the Messines Ridge, in a most welcome and significant joint act of remembrance of those of our countrymen who gave their lives in that war. Afterwards, as night begins to fall, I shall be present at the Menin Gate in Ypres where, every evening without fail, a **bugler** salutes those **Allied** soldiers who died on the fields of Northern Flanders.

'Age shall not weary them nor the years condemn. At the going down of the sun, and in the morning, we will remember them.'

Timeline

1914   28 June: Archduke Francis Ferdinand, heir to the throne of Austria-Hungary, and his wife Sofia, duchess of Hohenberg, are killed in Sarajevo.

28 July: Austria-Hungary declares war on Serbia.

1 August: Germany declares war on Russia.

3 August: Germany declares war on France.

4 August: Germany invades Belgium. Britain declares war on Germany.

5 August: Austria-Hungary declares war on Russia.

6 August: Serbia declares war on Germany

10 August: France and Britain declare war on Austria-Hungary.

12 August: Britain declares war on Austria-Hungary.

23 August: Battle of Mons begins.

5 September: First Battle of the Marne begins.

Mid October: First Battle of Ypres begins.

29 October: Turkey joins the **Central Powers**.

1 November: Russia declares war on Turkey

5 November: Britain and France declare war on Turkey.

1915   18 February: German submarine **blockade** of Britain begins.

22 March: Russian forces capture Przemysl.

22 April: Second Battle of Ypres begins. German troops use poison gas against Canadian troops at Ypres.

25 April: British forces land at Gallipoli.

7 May: The British liner *Lusitania* is sunk by a German U-boat.

23 May: Italy declares war on Austria-Hungary.

6 August: British forces land at Suvla Bay on the Gallipoli Peninsula.

20 December: British forces begin withdrawal from Gallipoli.

1916   21 February: Battle of Verdun begins.

24–29 April: Easter Uprising in Dublin

31 May–1 June: first Battle of Jutland

1 July: Battle of the Somme begins.

1917   15 March: Tsar Nicholas of Russia abdicates.

6 April: USA declares war on Germany.

6 November: October Revolution in Russia. Lenin comes to power and Russia becomes the USSR.

7 December: USA declares war on Austria-Hungary.

15 December: The Central Powers and Russia begin peace negotiations at Brest-Litovsk.

1918   3 March: The Central Powers and Russia sign peace treaty at Brest-Litovsk.

15 July: Second Battle of the Marne begins.

30 October: Turkey surrenders.

4 November: Austria-Hungary surrenders.

9 November: Kaiser Wilhelm II of Germany abdicates.

11 November: **Armistice** ends fighting.

Find out more

Books & websites

20th Century Perspectives: Key Battles of World War 1, David Taylor,
  (Heinemann Library, 2001)
20th Century Perspectives: Weapons and Technology of World War I,
  Paul Dowswell, (Heinemann Library, 2002)
The Causes of World War I, Tony Allan, (Heinemann Library, 2002).

www.heinemannexplore.co.uk
Go Exploring! Log onto Heinemann's online history resource.

www.historyteacher.net/APEuroCourse/ApEuro_Main_Weblinks_Page.htm
This site has a variety of primary sources and several sound files for downloading

www.spartacus.schoolnet.co.uk
Contains a huge amount of material about all aspects of World War I.

http://www.worldwar1.com
This site is devoted to all aspects of World War I.

List of primary sources

The author and publisher gratefully acknowledge the following publications and
websites from which written sources in the book are drawn. In some cases the
wording or sentence structure has been simplified to make the material more
appropriate for a school readership.

P.9 Franco-Russian Alliance Military Convention: www.yale.edu/lawweb/avalon/frrumil.htm
P.11 Borijove Jevtic: *The Faber Book of Reportage*: Ed John Carey (Faber & Faber, 1987)
P.13 Sergei N. Kurnakov: *The Faber Book of Reportage*: Ed John Carey (Faber & Faber, 1987)
P.15 Philip Gibbs: http://www.spartacus.schoolnet.co.uk/FWWaccredited.htm
P.17 Frederic Coleman: http://greatwar.topcities.com/First_Ypres/First_Ypres_01.htm
P.19 Private Donald Fraser: http://www.fordham.edu/halsall/mod/1918fraser.html
P.21 Bernard Pares: http://www.lib.byu.edu/~rdh/wwi/1915/przem.html
P.23 Samuel Weingott:
    http://www.minerva.com.au/austwardiary/warriors/Army/ww1/Gallipoli/sweingott.PDF
P.25 'Red Baron': www.richthofen.com/arcdocs/richt8.htm
P.27 Adolf K.G.E. von Spiegel: *The Faber Book of Reportage*: Ed John Carey (Faber & Faber, 1987)
P.29 James Stephens: http://indigo.ie/~1916/stephens.html
P.31 Ernest Francis: *The Faber Book of Reportage*: Ed John Carey (Faber & Faber, 1987)
P.33 Michael MacDonagh: *The Faber Book of Reportage*: Ed John Carey (Faber & Faber, 1987)
P.35 Sherwood Eddy: http://www.ku.edu/~libsite/wwi-www/Eddy/Eddy1.htm
P.37 William Pressey: *The Faber Book of Reportage*: Ed John Carey (Faber & Faber, 1987)
P.39 John Reed: *The Faber Book of Reportage*: Ed John Carey (Faber & Faber, 1987)
P.41 T.E. Lawrence: *The Faber Book of Reportage*: Ed John Carey (Faber & Faber, 1987)
P.43 Siegfried Sassoon: *Collected Poems* edited by Rupert Hart-Davis (Faber & Faber, 1999)
P.45 Robert Lindsay Mackay: http://www.greatwar.org/diaries/rlm9.htm
P.47 F.A. Voigt: http://greatwar4.topcities.com/War_is_Over/War_is_Over_01.htm
P.49 Harold Nicolson: *The Faber Book of Reportage*: Ed John Carey (Faber & Faber, 1987)
P.51 Queen Elizabeth II: Buckingham Palace Press Office
  http://www.royal.gov.uk/output/page231.asp

Glossary

A. 1.   first class

aerial   taking place in the air

aerodrome   airfield with hangars

airship   large, balloon-like aircraft

alliance   partnership agreed by two or more countries

Allied Powers   Great Britain and its empire, France, Belgium, Russia, Italy, the United States and their allies. Sometimes know as the Allies

ammunition   supply of bullets, shells and grenades

armistice   agreed stopping of fighting, especially the Armistice of 11 November 1918

assassinate   to murder someone, usually after careful planning

bandolier   belt containing bullets and worn over the shoulder

bearing   precise position of a ship or aircraft

bias   personal opinion that affects judgement

bill   draft of a proposed law

Black Maria   large shell that exploded with black smoke

blockading   preventing access to a place

Boche   insulting name for the Germans or Germany

bombardment   prolonged shelling

bow   the front part of a ship

bowline   rope or strap for attaching things on a ship

bridge   part of the ship where the captain and his officers navigate and command the ship

bugler   person who plays a bugle, a brass instrument similar to a small trumpet

bumph   papers and documents

carnage   terrible bloodshed

Central Powers   (Germany, Austria-Hungary, Bulgaria and Turkey

civilian   someone who is not a soldier

colonies   countries that are controlled by another nation

Commissar (in the Russian Revolution) an officer or person in a position of responsibility

communiqué   official message

communist   supporting a system of government in which the state (the government itself) owns all property and shares it among the people

conspirator   someone involved in a secret plan

convention   official agreement signed by many countries

delegation   group of representatives of a country

din   terribly loud noise

dressing station   place for giving emergency treatment to wounded soldiers

embankment   earth or stone bank

empire   group of nations ruled by another country

enlist   to join the armed forces willingly

flank   right or left side of an army

Fleet Street   street in London where newspapers traditionally have been based

front   long line formed by two opposing armies

gagged   with a piece of material held over the mouth to prevent speech

garrison   group of soldiers who protect a place

garrisoned   stationed for defensive purposes

gay   happy

haggard   rough-featured because of tiredness

Home Rule   chance for a country to look after many of its own affairs

Howeitat   Arab soldiers fighting against Turkish rule

howitzer   short gun

hullabaloo   loud commotion

Hun   insulting name for Germans

hussar   light-armed European cavalry soldier

immigrant   someone who settles in a new country

innocuous   appearing innocent

intermittent   occurring off and on

isolationist   opposing entry in a war that seems to have nothing to do with one's own country

League of Nations   group of countries to protect international peace

Lewis   type of machine-gun

looting   stealing from an abandoned building

mobilized   having prepared soldiers for war

morale   feelings (of hope and enthusiasm) towards an event

nationalism   desire to achieve independence

nationalist   someone who supports nationalism

NCO   non-commissioned officer

neutral   not involved with either side in a conflict

No Man's Land   area between two lines of trenches, controlled by neither side

parapet   earth or stone defence to protect soldiers

press   term to describe all newspapers, magazines and other written sources of news

primary source   original document or object from the past which helps us understand a historical event or era

projectile   object hurled in the air

propaganda   information designed to influence people's way of thinking

pungent   with a strong taste or smell

reconnaissance   military information gathering

reparations   payments made by a defeated nation after a war

reprieved   relieved or rescued

respirator   device to help breathing

respiratory   to do with breathing

revolution   widespread protest that overthrows a government

ricochet   (of a bullet), to bounce off an object and change direction

scabbard   sheath for a sword

secondary source   account based upon the evidence of past events

sentinel   someone who keeps watch

shell shock   form of mental illness that occurs after someone is exposed to terrible fighting

siege   prolonged attack (of a city or fortress)

sniper   person who fires shots from a hiding place

squadron   unit of ten to eighteen planes

stalemate   contest where neither side can win

Stokes gun   portable cannon

strategy   overall plan

stricken   overcome with misfortune or illness

switch line   hastily dug trench filled with armed soldiers

testament   writings that act as witness to an event

Teuton   one of the earliest settlers in what is now Germany

treaty   agreement between nations

Triple Alliance   pre-war alliance of Germany, Austria-Hungary and Italy

Triple Entente   pre-war alliance of Great Britain, France and Russia

turret   low tower for a gun and gunners on a ship

usher   person who shows people to their seats at a gathering

Verey lights   signal lights used in warfare

volunteer   person who enrols for unpaid military service

Index